THE EROTICS OF GOD

The Erotics of God

The soul of sweet delight can never be defil'd

Sebastian Barker

Published 2005
by

Smokestack Books
PO Box 408, Middlesbrough TS5 6WA
Tel : 01642 813997
e-mail : info@smokestack-books.co.uk
www.smokestack-books.co.uk

Copyright Sebastian Barker 2005
All rights reserved

Cover design and print by
James Cianciaruso
j.cianciaruso@ntlworld.com

Cover: The sculpture by Lorenzo Bernini.
Death of the Blessed Ludovica Albertoni,
detail, marble, 1675.
In the Altieri Chapel, San Francesco a Ripa, Rome.
Photograph by David Finn.
Photograph of Sebastian Barker
by John Minihan.

ISBN 0-9548691-6-8

Smokestack Books
gratefully acknowledges the support of
Middlesbrough Borough Council
and Arts Council North East.

Smokestack Books is a member of
Independent Northern Publishers
www.northernpublishers.co.uk

Dedicated to Peter & Diana Carter

Acknowledgements

Grateful acknowledgements are made to the editors for the following: 'Epithalamion', 'Walk With Me' in *Acumen:* 'The Articles of Prayer', 'The Elderberry Tree', 'The Fluting Trumpeteer' in *Poetry Wales:* 'Drops On A Thread' in *Kindred Spirit:* 'Springtime In The Greek Mountains' in *The Road to Parnassus: Homage to Peter Russell on his 75th Birthday,* University of Salzburg; and 'On The Labours Of A Literary Friend' in *A Glass of New Made Wine*, University of Salzburg.

I

The Erotics of God

The Lyrics   Page

Epithalamion 12
The Conscience Of The Real 14
Walk With Me 15
O Blackbird 16
The Robin Of My Days 17
The Fluting Trumpeteer 18
Good Morning, Moon 19
Good Morning, Moon 19
The Son Of Man 20
The Elderberry Tree 22
The Articles Of Prayer 23
Old Nick 24
No Hope In Termites 25
The Deeper Deep 26
I Cannot Tell You How The Greek 27
Naïvety's The Strongest Force 29
The Martial Contract 30
The Lonesome Jaguar 31
Sun On Summer Wheat 32
The Mountain Top 33
The Girl Alive To Asphodels 34
The Nuthoods 35
When Gandhi Came 36
The Insubstantial Feel 37
Bend On Rotten Knees 38
Erotic Impulse 39
Rosaceous Wonders 40
The Stranger In The Pass 41
The Reflection 42

The Exegesis 44

Spirit of the River

Page

Springtime In The Greek Mountains 54
On The Labours Of A Literary Friend 56
For Eddie Linden On His 70th Birthday............ 58
For Glyn Hughes On His 70th Birthday 59
The Bower Of Bliss 60
Jubilee 2002 62
Larkin.. 64
Dickhead 66
The Burial Of The Christian Hypocrites............ 67
A Song For Saint Peter.. 68
What The Statues Saw 69
Drops On A Thread 70
When Do You Sleep? 72
Untitled 73
Spirit Of The River 74

Notes to 'Spirit of the River'............................... 76

EPIGRAPH

THE EROTICS OF GOD. ORIGEN (*c.* 185-*c.* 254), theologian, philosopher, biblical exegete. Pupil of Clement of Alexandria. A skilled linguist and translator, Origen noticed the Greek version of the Song of Songs frequently used the relatively uncommon word for love, *agape*, rather than the common word, *eros*. Taking the two to be the same and drawing on the Song, he likened the relationship between God and a person to one in which the word of God is the groom, and the church or the individual soul is the bride. The idea had currency in earlier traditions, such as the interpretation of the Song as an allegory of God's love for Israel, or in Paul's letter to the Ephesians 5:29-32 ('This is a great mystery, and I am applying it to Christ and the church.') The idea was taken up in the Christian tradition, by Bernard of Clairvaux and Richard Rolle for example, to the extent that by the 14th century the lyric poem *Quia Amore Langueo* was at ease with Christ's love for mankind as something as majestic and profound as erotic love (in the common meaning of the term) but substantially more than it. The writings of Teresa of Avila and John of the Cross in the 16th century continued the tradition.

So the erotics of God is to the erotics of the person as the erotics of the person is to the erotics of the insect. Those who have observed the mating of dragonflies will not underestimate the last.

Modern scholars who have published on the erotics of God, as an established subject in university education, include Anders Nygren *Agape & Eros* (1953), John M. Rist *Eros & Psyche: Studies in Plato, Plotinus & Origen* (1964), Henryk Pietras *L'amore in Origene* (1988), Roland E. Murphy *The Song of Songs* (1990), Catherine Osborne *Eros Unveiled: Plato and the God of Love* (1994), and Joseph W. Trigg *Origen* (1998).

If eros is the conduit in love between men and women, the erotics of God is the conduit in love between God and mankind, with Christ as the mediator in the Christian system of belief. So if we can say the erotics of God is brought into being *ab initio* by faithful obedience to the first and greatest commandment, You shall love the Lord your God with all your heart, mind, soul, and strength, Deuteronomy 6:4-9, Matthew 22:37-38, the subject may be understood as the natural consequence of faith.

The Erotics of God

A Poem

The soul of sweet delight can never be defil'd

With an Exegesis

Epithalamion

Immortal God's almighty eyes
Enclose and light the starry skies.

By day the luminary sun
Instructs us in our union.

Take my hand and lead me to
The country of my love for you.

Walk me down the sacred aisle
Resurrection in your smile.

Let love interpret what the mind
In all its rancour cannot find.

Tie the living spirit with
The supersilky thongs of love.

Consecrated by the word
Display it in the house of God.

When I lift my eyelids, blink
All the world in what you think.

Reciprocal ecstatic law
We practice to be two no more.

Let music sound the mighty chord
Praise the human soul adored.

Enrol the sanctity of these
Standing in the ancient pews.

I see a village, where the sun
Dandles on thatch the holy one

Of Ramsbury. He is the word
As fortunate as those who've heard

Him calling from the rooftops, where
The trees articulate the air.

'O eros of the promised land
Take O take me by the hand.'

The Conscience Of The Real

Alone, alone, alone no more,
    I roam the loamy earth,
Chloë tree and rooky caw
    bringing life to birth.

Clouds melt, the awakening dream
    coming true, to heal
Dread of solitude, redeem
    the conscience of the real.

I walk with you in love so great
    the spring of glory is.
O sun of March illuminate
    the vehicles of bliss!

Walk With Me

Tread softly, tread the marshy grass
    suns lick from the plate
Of being, tread all things that pass
    to the immaculate.

Tread the logic of the stars,
    the surface of the moon,
The fiery light of city bars
    on the paving stone.

Tread the stories told to make
    heaven out of lies
And truthful men and women break
    in love's ecstatic cries.

Walk with me, the word is hot,
    the doctor of the sane.
I've walked the world and what I've got
    is music on the brain.

O Blackbird

O blackbird on my green green lawn –
    viriditas the term –
It is my office to describe
    the banquet of the worm.

So black in bladed tuck, you pick
    your way along the grass,
Perfect in your understated
    deadly consciousness.

Like fighter jets which cut the sky
    with pointed human will,
You are my education in
    the trimness of the kill.

The Robin Of My Days

Today, today, of all I sing
    no other will I praise
More than the robin redbreast,
    the robin of my days.

So rock with me and sway the way
    a robin hits the branch
And bounces on the seeming bliss
    of God's sweet avalanche.

The Fluting Trumpeteer

Upon the very drop of night
    death, nor being is.
It is spectacular to see
    the mental consequences.

There is no follow-up to truth,
    death in the engine lies.
Don't give me resurrection, give me
    the truth of my demise.

No more, no longer, death has come
    to whom it'd never left.
Nor am I circumscribed by this,
    nor in truth bereft.

I am the sum of all I am
    breathing God's good cheer,
Happy to be alive, to be
    his fluting trumpeteer.

Good Morning, Moon

Good morning, moon, the night was hard,
    the night was hard and long.
Good morning, moon, the night was hard,
    the night was hard and long.

I saw the stars, o moon, but they
    did not notice me.
I saw the stars, o moon, but they
    did not notice me.

How come the morning comes, o moon,
    how come the morning comes?
How come the morning comes, o moon,
    how come the morning comes?

From God's ecstatic forces   light
    the traitor of the mind
Considers wrong, o man, is right,
    the seer is the blind.

The Son Of Man

Don't come to me
 with talk of love,
The state's
 prolific book.
I have the subjects
 off by heart,
But take a closer look.

Across the rivers
 of the sea
Came God's
 erotic charge,
And in the
 affidavit proved
The ecstasy at large.

Below the bottom
 of the sea,
Above the wheels
 of time,
The heart of hearts
 came challenging
The art of the sublime.

And in the picture
    painted true
The truth
    which I observed:
The son of man
    advances in
The beauty of the word.

There is no truth
    nor beauty more,
More than the mightiest:
    the son of man
Comes journeying
    in ecstasy
And rest.

The Elderberry Tree

What crisis in my splitting brain –
    the officer knows this.
I can't forget the lovely rain
    when all the world was bliss.

The droplets on the petals bounced
    like hope's substantial plea,
But in that greenery announced
    the end of being me.

No terror, no conclusive blues,
    no presupposing law:
The tax of being claims its dues
    to give and to withdraw.

The rain came down like bullets on
    the elderberry tree.
I watched almighty God become
    the better part of me.

The Articles Of Prayer

Wake, the day has not begun,
    let the sleeping sleep.
The first light from the rheumy sun
    emerges from the deep.

The draught we drank is gone, the ones
    we drank it with are dead.
We touched the moon and now it slowly
    circulates our bed.

Talk to me of times gone by,
    the all translating wine,
And on the bosom of the dawn
    teach me the divine.

Slowly, slowly, rich with choice,
    caress me with your care,
And in the elocution voice
    the articles of prayer.

Old Nick

I die by day, by day, but you
    neither die nor end,
Immortal in your arrogance,
    the politician's friend.

Like chocolate tipped into a cup
    to fill an empty brain,
You talk to me of sweetness, shit
    I'm flushing down the drain.

Death laughs in your face, Old Nick,
    you do not see her smile,
The cunning angel, arm in arm,
    who walks you down the aisle.

No Hope In Termites

No hope in termites, tetchy shade,
    no hope in being kind,
No hope in rubber bullets made
    the eyesight of the blind.

I walk the very edge of life
    shot by what is true,
And in my dying to my wife
    report the news that's new.

The apple grows within the tree,
    the vine matures with grace,
And in the upshot, I am me
    in love's uncertain place.

The poem knows no natural bound,
    the preternatural force
Lost in spinal whirlwinds found
    in sexual intercourse.

The Deeper Deep

Nowhere to go, nowhere to hide,
    death has come, my friend.
I know the truth, the truth that lied,
    the death that came to end.

Oh yes, the victory of love
    was short, but shorter yet
The victory of death   enough
    it was not ultimate.

The glory of the thing that made
    the instance of the first
Became the subtlety betrayed,
    the worse within the worst.

So rock with me and cradle down,
    there is no sweeter sleep,
Love and death continuum
    within the deeper deep.

I Cannot Tell You How The Greek

I'll mark it right and write it true,
   the triumph of the brain.
I saw the opposition end,
   it will not end again.
Despair as deep as being is
   the thing that's troubling me.
The depth of our delusion is
   the deepest we can see.

I saw the sun at midnight burn
   the triumph of the brain
Clean out of me and leaving there
   the vacuum of pain.
Despair as deep as being sings
   a melancholy song.
I'll mark it right and write it true,
   the triumph of the wrong.

Yet thoughtful, for the time has come
   for dying – take my chair –
And in the Greek elysium
   remember I was there.
I was the undergraduate,
   I was the quirky don,
And in the middle of the night
   I was the thoughtful one.

I cannot tell you how the Greek
    within my temples burns
The fires of God as melancholy
    as their many pains.
I cannot tell you how the Greek
    restores me to my art.
It suffers in the fires and finds
    the tempered steel of heart.

Naïvety's The Strongest Force

Naïvety's the strongest force
    to filch a poet's mind.
Net and butterfly, of course,
    the language double bind.

Three thousand years are not enough
    to learn the poet's trade.
What is a poet thinking of
    to make the thing that's made?

Naïvety, a reflex nod,
    guarantees the word
Constructs a plaster cast of God
    less witty than absurd.

Naïvety, like fashion, fakes
    a castle in the air.
We enter with the queens and dukes
    to find there's nothing there.

The Martial Contract

Search me, I'm alive to death,
    alive to living too,
Alive to love's worst irony:
    it's killing me and you.

We breathe and breathless breathe no more,
    the oxygen desèrts
The sandy blizzards where we come
    to learn the martial arts.

About as useless as a prayer
    chanted on the roof
Of Noah's Ark beneath the waves,
    we cling to certain proof.

The only certainty is this:
    nothing is so free
As God almighty to abandon
    my lover's heart and me.

I pray the way my lover's heart
    is God's own lover's way
Of teaching me the martial art
    of dying, how to say

I am my lover's heart and she
    is God's as God's is mine
And in the martial contract we
    wake up to this and sign.

The Lonesome Jaguar

O Chloë, no one knows how you
    came to be or are,
In London's jungle, black and blue,
    the lonesome jaguar.

You prowl the jungle, in your head
    attuned to every blade
Of grass, of wit, of steel, to read
    the intricate displayed.

In it, lounging on, it's true,
    the girder of a tree,
I am the better part of you
    the better part of me.

Sun On Summer Wheat

Miranda, in your jadeblue eyes,
    I find you happy there,
To soothe me, as your hands arise
    to brush your golden hair.

Let my *papa's* thought become
    the driver of your brain.
We pass through parishes to some
    household of the sane.

Religious are they, folk who sleep
    through time as hard as rock,
Like you and me, because they keep
    the vigil of the clock.

They labour like the incandescent
    sun on summer wheat,
And rise and shine, for time is spent
    making it replete.

The Mountain Top

My son, my son, I see you on
    the mountain top alone,
Your arms aloft, the terror gone,
    the great achievement done.

The mountain is a crown of stone,
    below a perfect one.
Allow me if I proudly own
    the title of my son.

Take it, shake it, throw it over
    the mountainside to see
It boomerang the world to hover
    over you not me.

The rain of time comes down like tears,
    there is no stopping it.
We learn, O God, how life appears
    on mountains topping it.

The Girl Alive To Asphodels

The horse has consciousness you find
    a girl of thirteen feeding his
Consciousness in mind.

The village round about is green,
    a house of stone is looking down
Where Hitler's army's been.

The trees are hung with fruit and the
    sky's as sapphire as the blue sea is
Shimmering with light within her.

The radar of the horse propels,
    over fields, between the stones,
The girl alive to asphodels.

A chainsaw cuts some logs in half,
    the sun is looking down the hill
On Hitler's epitaph.

The Nuthoods

Break the bread, and break it well,
    the nuthoods have arrived.
Forgive me if I skirmish round
    the homes through which they've drived.

They've driven through the newborn face,
    they've driven through the womb,
They've driven through the act of love
    in any living room.

Forgive me if I listen to
    the resurrected dead.
I need them in my proclamation
    to hear what they have said.

'We are the nuthoods of the dead,
    we are a sober class,
We were the nuthoods of the world,
    before we came to pass.

The nuthoods fear no consequence
    in hell, they're those you'll meet
As ordinary and as kind
    on any suburb street.

What is it they set out to do?
    God knows and so do we.
They want to rule the world and make it
    a better place to be.

They live in hell by force of will,
    they run the national race
Usurping God, a big mistake,
    with nothing in its place.'

When Gandhi Came

When Gandhi came,
    an empire rolled,
As suspect as its shame
    the bullets told.

When Gandhi came,
    no soldier knew
How to act or blame,
    the women too.

When Gandhi came,
    the world was young,
There was a moral aim,
    and that was sung.

When Gandhi came,
    what Hitler said
Was nothing like the same.
    He shot them dead.

When Gandhi came,
    the world was old,
Older than his fame,
    the story cold.

The Insubstantial Feel

Get out of bed, get down to work,
    get on with something real.
I've had it up to here with you,
    the insubstantial feel.

Is there nothing you can do
    to write your poetry
More like something I can read
    than damn you for, for free?

So lonely on the bank of time,
    I'm rotting to your verse,
But in its music I can hear
    the rattle of my curse.

There's nothing in you. I have come
    to raze you to the ground.
You are what I, you are what you,
    in witlessness have found.

Bend On Rotten Knees

Bend on rotten knees, protest
    I was ordered to,
I was ordered to the feast
    of killing. Was it you?

It was me. Your rotten knees
    desecrate the scale
of *sapiens*, if you please.
    I know your orders well.

I was the bullet which you slipped
    so neatly in my back.
I was the africano shipped
    in stack, in stack, in stack.

I want no answer from your can,
    you are the waste of time.
You are the antidote of man.
    I am what I am.

Erotic Impulse

Erotic impulse speak to me
    and be the poem's heart.
I want to know what you can see
    within the sacred art.

Show me all the golden rules
    to educate my eye.
Show me all the porno spools
    I neither want nor why.

'I'll speak if you will listen now
    I have the upper hand.
I am the itch to love and how,
    if you can understand.

I am the impulse to be free
    within the source of bliss,
The impulse to be loved and stately,
    ecstatically this.'

Rosaceous Wonders

Tread the cottage grapes to wine,
    ascend the cellar stair,
Sit down with me tonight and dine,
    there is a purpose here.

I knew you in the days before
    we had our stab at being wise.
The rain falls on the roof, the floor
    comes as no surprise.

Tell me, did you learn a thing
    or two, or did the blood
Prohibit consubstantial learning,
    a vicious abstinence your mood?

See the trees provide the flower
    forgiving what we all have done,
Administer the simple power
    of roses in the garden sun.

O rosaceous wonders on
    the gilt of evening, speak to me,
And be the understanding gone
    from lilacs, perfect artistry.

The Stranger In The Pass

Sunlight on a broken fence,
    sparrows in the grass,
The wheels of industry make sense,
    the stranger in the pass.

What is it, stranger, what do you
    want? 'I want to live
Before I die, an overview,
    a rich alternative.'

Amazing swans fly like the truth
    difficult to believe.
The city traffic's heading south,
    there's summer in the breeze.

Ten to one the sky is blue,
    the picnics in the wood
Conceal the witty families who
    have long since understood.

To live before you die, attend,
    O stranger in the pass,
The cracks within the family mend,
    sparrows in the grass.

The Reflection

The crazy sky is slit with light,
    the dream emerges from
The vast receptacle of night
    where no attendants came.

Slit from ear to ear the brain
    sees itself in this,
The crazy colours of the sun
    exploding the abyss.

The Exegesis

Epigraph on title page. William Blake, 'The Marriage of Heaven & Hell', Plate 9.

12. 'Epithalamion'. *Immortal God* refers to the idea of God found in the work called *The Instructor*, by Clement of Alexandria *(c.* 150-*c.* 215 AD). In this work, Clement lays out the idea of God and the word of God as the Pedagogue, the Teacher, the Educator, the Instructor, from whom the prophets, poets, artists, doctors, and teachers receive their vocations and all the important details of these vocations. Clement's work as a church father has its roots in Greek philosophy and, more importantly, Judaism. *the luminary sun / Instructs*: the idea of the Instructor may be glimpsed in the stars at night; by day, the idea may be glimpsed in the luminary sun. *The luminary sun* echoes the luminary son of God, as well as the luminous physical sun of nature. Both are extensions of the Instructor. *The luminary sun* of the Instructor instructs the man and the woman in their union. This is something to be celebrated in *the house of God*. *Resurrection in your smile* invokes the fact that in Christian theology the baptised person takes on the kingly, priestly, and prophetic offices of the system of belief. These declare unanimously that the downgrading of the person through the sin and the death of the body is countered, refuted, and redeemed by the upgrading of the person through the resurrection or the anastasis of the body. Naturally, in the sacrament of marriage, the bride and the groom, instructed in the offices of the system of belief, walk the road to the resurrection of the body rather than the road to the sin and the death of the body. *Ramsbury*, the wedding of bride and groom takes place in the church Holy Cross in the village of Ramsbury in Wiltshire. In Saxon times, Ramsbury had a cathedral and an archbishop, three of whom went on to become Archbishops of Canterbury. However, any other appropriate place may be substituted. The lyric may be spoken by bride and groom in any combination of lines or couplets. *the holy one*, who is *the word*, is Christ the Messiah, who comes to us in the present (see the notes about time in 'The Son Of Man' and 'Sun On Summer Wheat'). The final couplet is spoken by the officiating priest as the representative of the Instructor.

14. 'The Conscience Of The Real'. *alone no more* because married in the eyes of the Instructor. *chloë*, a term for the first green showings of spring. *the awakening dream* is an allusion to 'The Imagination may be compared to Adam's dream – he awoke and found it truth.' (John Keats, letter to Benjamin Bailey, 22 Nov 1817). Keats is himself referring to John Milton's *Paradise*

Lost, book 8, lines 460-490, in which Adam dreams of Eve. When he wakes up, he sees her coming towards him 'Led by her Heav'nly Maker'. *dread of solitude* refers to absence from God as well as to absence from the loved one. *conscience of the real* refers to awareness of the reality of God and the reality of the loved one. *the vehicles of bliss!* are the manifestations of spring, when interpreted as the glory of God and the loved one. *the vehicles* relate to many other ideas and images in the work as a whole, especially *The fiery light of city bars / on the paving stone* in 'Walk With Me', *sun on summer wheat* in 'Sun On Summer Wheat', the *rosaceous wonders* and the *lilacs* in 'Rosaceous Wonders', and *The crazy colours of the sun* in 'The Reflection'.

15. 'Walk With Me'. Tread softly, W.B. Yeats (1865-1939), 'Tread softly because you tread on my dreams', from his poem 'He Wishes for the Cloths of Heaven' (1899). *the plate / of being* refers to the ground of being in presocratic philosophy. *the logic of the stars* refers to Doctor Johnson (1709-1784) on Isaac Watts (1674-1748): 'And who has taught the art of reasoning and the science of the stars? Even Isaac Watts.' *to make / heaven out of lies*, is to create the erotics of God out of the world of lies, which, by contrast, creates the descent into the abyss. *the word is hot, / the doctor of the sane* refers to the word of the Instructor as the doctor bringing us round from unconsciousness to sanity.

16. 'O Blackbird'. *viriditas* is a term made our property by Hildegard of Bingen (1098-1179); and, before her, by Gregory the Great (c. 540-604). It refers to the green light of nature which appears, particularly to artists, to be divine. Theologically, it is the gift of the holy spirit, having life and strength. This is a tie-up with *chloë* in the second lyric, 'The Conscience Of The Real'. The blackbird kills, reminding us that there is nothing sentimental about the erotics of God in its recognition of nature. In his poem 'The Garden', Andrew Marvell (1621-1678) wrote the enigmatic couplet, 'Annihilating all that's made / To a green Thought in a green Shade.' In this lyric, *viriditas* and the 'green Thought in a green Shade' are taken to be one and the same thing.

17. 'The Robin Of My Days'. *seeming bliss* because the divine is not something which can be encapsulated and turned into data by the human mind.

18. 'The Fluting Trumpeteer'. *the engine* refers to the human body and its mortality. *Don't give me resurrection* is one of the *mental consequences* of *death* and the nullity of *being*. *fluting* is an oblique reference to the flute and what it signifies in 'Johann Joachim Quantz's Five Lessons', the poem by W.S. Graham (1918-1986).

19. 'Good Morning Moon'. *the night was hard / the night was hard and long* is a re-writing of a line from the poem 'The Watcher on the Tower' by Madison Julius Cawein (1865-1914), which has 'The Night was dark; the Night was dark and long.' Lines are repeated, because they are spoken by man and woman in turn. In the final stanza, the moon addresses them both together as *o man*, as in humankind. *the traitor of the mind* is a personification of evil, of sin.

20. 'The Son Of Man'. *The state's / prolific book* refers to both what is written about the state of love and what is written about the political philosophy of the state or the republic. *take a closer look*, so as not to be complacent about knowledge of love and knowledge of political philosophy. *affidavit*, the written statement of the Instructor. *proved*, such as we find in the Song of Songs, which is part of the written statement. *The art of the sublime* refers to notions of the sublime suggested in the Greek critical treatise by Longinus, *On the Sublime* (1st century AD), and Edmund Burke (1729-1797) in his work *A Philosophical Enquiry into the Sublime and the Beautiful*. The idea in the lyric is that *God's / erotic charge* challenges these notions. In the erotic charge, we find *The son of man / advances in / The beauty of the word*. The sublimity of Longinus and Edmund Burke cannot be said to compare with the sublimity – the grandeur, the terror, and the beauty – with which the Instructor appears to and addresses Ezekiel in the book of Ezekiel. *son of man* (sometimes rendered 'mortal') is the form of address used by God to Ezekiel. It is also the form of address used by Jesus of Nazareth to refer to himself in his ministry as the Messiah, the Christ. It is important in this lyric, as in 'Epithalamion', to recognise that an aspect of Christianity perceives Christ or the Messiah as coming to us from the past, hence the use of the AD dating system, whereas an aspect of Judaism (Messianism) perceives Christ or the Messiah as coming to us from the future, hence the use of the expression 'Moshiach is coming'. In the lyric, *God's / erotic charge* comes to us *Above the wheels / of time*; it comes to us *journeying* in the present. This is

an attempt to unite aspects of Judaism and Christianity.

22. 'The Elderberry Tree'. *the officer* refers to the officer class in war, the *crisis* in the official mind being the simultaneous presence in it of the remembrance of love and the imminence of death. *blues* refers to songs in this genre, *conclusive* because they celebrate hopelessness. *presupposing law*, in practising philosophy, that is to say the príma philosophía, one of the great errors is to presuppose anything to be true, a law especially. *to give and to withdraw*, it is axiomatic in Heideggerian philosophy that being comes into existence, gives us the world, goes out of existence, takes the world away from us. Likewise, in facing being as in facing art, we give our understanding to them and withdraw our understanding from them in the spirit of reverence, not in the spirit of analytical dissection or detached dominance.

23. 'The Articles Of Prayer'. *the divine* and *the articles of prayer* refer to the teachings of the Instructor.

24. 'Old Nick'. The name is a term for the devil, or the personification of evil, or sin. *Death laughs* in the *face* of Old Nick because death betrays sin in their marriage. This marriage is the obverse of the marriage in 'Epithalamion'. *the politician's friend* is a reference to John Webster (c. 1578-c. 1632) in his play *The Duchess of Malfi* (act 3 scene 2 lines 321-323), 'A politician is the devil's quilted anvil, / He fashions all sins on him, and the blows / Are never heard.'

25. 'No Hope In Termites'. *termites* is a reference to termite man in John Boorman's film *The Emerald Forest*, in which humankind is divided into three types. These are the Beautiful People, who are kindly and drink spiritual drinks to enter the spirit world; the Dangerous People, who are ruthless and cannibalistic; both of whom live in the forest. And the Termite People, who live everywhere else. Termite man is the archetypal clockwork man oblivious to the consequences of actions and blind to the *viriditas* of God and nature. *tetchy shade* because termite man is always tetchy at rest, not relaxed. *the news that's new*, refers to Ezra Pound (1885-1972), 'Literature is news that stays news', *The ABC of Reading* (1934). The poem is not *natural* in the sense that it is *preternatural* or more than natural. *spinal whirlwinds* refer to the currents of sexual energy in contact with the erotics

of God as well as the conception of the person.

26. 'The Deeper Deep'. *the thing that made / the instance of the first* is the Instructor or God or the ground of being. This is the 'I am that I am' whose linguistic roots are in the Hebraic verb 'hayah' 'to be' in Exodus 3:14. The idea recurs in the lyric 'Bend On Rotten Knees'. *the subtlety betrayed* is the transformation of *the instance of the first* into *the worse within the worst*, the transformation of good into evil. It is also an echo of the sonnet by Gerard Manley Hopkins (1844-1889), 'No worst, there is none.' *continuum*, derived from 'How readily would we become / The seamless live continuum / Of supple and coherent stuff, / Whose form is truth, whose content love', W.H. Auden (1907-1973), in his poem 'New Year Letter'.

27. 'I Cannot Tell You How The Greek'. *the opposition* refers to evil. The poem sees the *end* of this. Then immediately its reappearance; and *it will not end again. Despair as deep as being* comes into existence with this recognition. We see no further than our delusions. Suicide seems an appropriate response. But the sun at midnight, found in poems by Joseph Mary Plunkett (1887-1916), David Gascoyne (1916-2001), and Aidan Andrew Dun, erases suicidal consideration, cleaning out the mind, but nevertheless still leaving the vacuum of pain. No advance. Wrong triumphs over right. What is the cure for the melancholy song? Neither *the Greek elysium*, nor the teaching taught to the *undergraduate* by *the quirky don*, however *thoughtful* because *the time has come / for dying*. Melancholy is cured by the teachings of Instructor, who teaches the tempering of the spirit in the fires of affliction or the transubstantiation of pain in the system of belief.

29. 'Naïvety's The Strongest Force'. This refers to the unconscious element in poetic practice. Not the unconscious in the Jungian sense, which is something living and from which we derive our consciousness, but unconscious in the normal sense of being unaware. Naïve poetic practice is unaware of its responsibilities. Study of at least *three thousand years* of poetic practice is the minimum, the lyric says, to form an idea of these responsibilities. *to make the thing that's made*, the obverse of *the thing that made / the instance of the first* in 'The Deeper Deep'.

30. 'The Martial Contract'. *love's worst irony: / it's killing me and you*, the erotics of God in sexual intercourse, which gives rise to the generation of the person, seems also to give rise, therefore, to the death of the person. On the face of it, the erotics of God is nothing other than the erotics of life and death. However, the lyric posits the martial contract of the relationship between the lovers as continuous with the existence of God as the core of the joint system of belief. At the end of the lyric, both of them sign up to this contract. Nevertheless, the lyric also recognises the constituency of God possesses the right of being absolutely free from any humanly-imposed concern about the lovers or the rest of us whatsoever. *nothing is so free / As God almighty to abandon* – not only *my lover's heart and me* but also the world in which we live. The transition from such presence to such absence of God, and vice versa, turns on the expression *I pray*. The title of the lyric is an anagram of 'the marital contract'.

31. 'The Lonesome Jaguar'. The *chloë* of the second lyric has grown into *Chloë* in London's jungle, this being the city of man not the city of God. *Chloë* and her father meet in London. *the intricate displayed* is her vision of the city. He is a lonesome jaguar too, *lounging on... / the girder of a tree*. The lyric is addressed to my daughter, Chloë.

32. 'Sun On Summer Wheat'. *papa's thought* is paternal thought for a daughter but also *papa's thought* where *papa* is the Greek for an Orthodox priest. *household of the sane*, an institution in which religious make their home. Religious is the term for people who keep *the vigil of the clock*. They do not let time dominate the sacred vocation. On the contrary. They work *like sun on summer wheat* to harrow *time as hard as rock*. They bring into being the *wheat* of the bread which gives meaning to *time*. *Time* is *replete* in the *summer wheat*; and vice versa, the *summer wheat* is replete in *time*. The lyric is addressed to my daughter, Miranda.

33. 'The Mountain Top'. *My son my son*, an echo of 'O Absalom, my son, my son', 2 Samuel 18:33. The mountain is both real and imaginary. On it, father and son receive and understand the reciprocation of their relationship. The consummation of this understanding is the life of God *topping* the reality of grief and time. The lyric is addressed to my son, Daniel.

34. 'The Girl Alive To Asphodels'. Animals possess consciousness in the way the featherless biped man possesses consciousness. For some reason, girls and horses are, in this respect, particularly aware of conscious rapport with each other. Hitler's army is at variance with this, an extreme example of termite man in destructive function. The consciousness of the girl and the horse are seen as an expansion of consciousness; the consciousness of termite man as a diminution of it. The lyric is addressed to my daughter, Xanthi.

35. 'The Nuthoods'. These are the termite men. They think nothing of bulldozing towns and villages while families are in the buildings. They speak from the dead to explain their actions. They are the ideologues of the political philosophy of the nation state, which has usurped all consideration of God and the power of God. *a big mistake*. This is the identification man makes with his own power over and above the power of nature and the power of God. I call this <u>*the Heideggerian mistake*</u> after the gross identification Heidegger (1889-1976) made in the 1930s between the Nazi cause and the reality of such natural and divine power. He made the Nazi cause, natural and supernatural power, one and the same thing. He came to understand his mistake, however; and was cleared by the Allied Forces from any serious involvement with the Nazis. All his major and exemplary philosophical work on being and time indicate the staggering scale of his mistake. This becomes, in the work as a whole, symbolic of the human slide into the fall of man.

36. 'When Gandhi Came'. Gandhi and the moral force behind him helped to topple the British Empire. But his approach would not have seen off the termite man of the Third Reich. *the story cold*, the times got colder, as they have done before.

37. 'The Insubstantial Feel'. An attack on vacuity in poetry and art.

38. 'Bend On Rotten Knees'. An attack on mindless carrying out of orders, set in distinction from the teachings of the Instructor, the *I am what I am*.

39. 'Erotic Impulse'. The impulse speaks in the third and fourth stanzas to establish eros as nothing pornographic but the *itch*, the urge, the *impulse* to love.

40. 'Rosaceous Wonders'. *the blood*, the blood consequent upon the fall of man. *Prohibit consubstantial learning*, did the fall of man prohibit the learning of the teaching of the Instructor? The learning is *consubstantial* because in the teaching of the Instructor the trinity of Father, Son, and Holy Spirit are said to be of one substance or homo-ousios or *consubstantial* with each other. *vicious abstinence* is the power of puritanical thinking, the inverse of which is violence. Nietzsche (1844-1900) identified such *vicious abstinence* as the key psychological feature of the ascetic priest, especially in *On the Genealogy of Morals* (1887), 'Third Essay: What is the Meaning of Ascetic Ideals?' In this essay, he gives us, in a most prescient way, the clearest possible forerunner and character portrait of Adolf Hitler. *the simple power / of roses in the garden sun* is a recognition of our preference for the erotics of God over and above *the Heideggerian mistake*. *rosaceous wonders*, the wonders of the *Rosaceae* family of plants and trees to which the rose, the cherry, the hawthorn, the crab, the rowan, and the pear belong. *the understanding gone* is the slide into *the Heideggerian mistake.* The lyric restores understanding to the perfect artistry of *lilacs* as well as to *perfect artistry* itself.

41. 'The Stranger In The Pass'. *The stranger* is the person from outside the participation mystique of the general consensus. *The stranger* comes to the consensus for wisdom about how to live with the knowledge of death. The lyric reveals and conceals this wisdom in the mending of family bonds and all that such mending implies. The mending, coming as it does from the Instructor, also has the power to mend *sparrows in the grass*. As in 'Are not two sparrows sold for a penny? Yet not one of them will fall to the ground apart from your Father.' Matthew 10:29.

42. 'The Reflection'. *the dream*, a reference back to *the awakening dream* of the second lyric, 'The Conscience Of The Real'. Hell on earth, *The vast receptacle of night / where no attendants came* – *the Heideggerian mistake* writ large – is exploded by the power of God and the erotics of God, *the crazy colours of the sun*.

II

Spirit of the River

Springtime In The Greek Mountains

For Peter Russell on his 75th birthday
'We've cast grace out of our life; that's what we lack.' (George Seferis)

I came to grace but grace came not to me
    (the lone isles sleeping in the sea's unrest)
Elusive as the dawn now dawn has ceased to be.
    O give me grace, I pray, but grace has long progressed.
Do not be trite, I plead, for grace is rare,
    and I, though dark, her worthy courtier.

Silence, like music, now air that must contend
    with all that is, is not, yet will be heard.
Easy to speak, they say. Not so, dear friend.
    To speak is to carve and not to be absurd.
The night is always with us, and the day,
    lit by the sun, in which we go astray.

No deed or thought so rich as that which brings
    peace without frontiers to a poor man's son.
Get back in line, the argument is spring's:
    I am the thought in which the deed is done.
Beyond the moon, colossal sparks in space
    conceal the spark of all, incandescent grace.

What of it? Nothing. Guess. The room is still.
    The light bulb's incandescence is an arch of thought
Through which we travel, the walls a miracle.
    Even as the air we breathe is nothing bought.
My table, hewn from pine, offers you this clue:
    my mind creates the shapes, the shapes are you.

Books closed. A glass of wine. The yellow air
    breathing the beauty of high German art:
Beethoven, carving the silence to a silent prayer.
    May we too do as much before we too depart.
And in this hope no quantum leaps remain.
    Give back to life, whose grace has made us sane.

Easy to begin, not so to close,
    the lone isles sleeping in the sea's unrest.
Grace to be born, grace to enjoy repose,
    but hell to be in heaven by hell possessed.
How do we come, our progress all too slow,
    to know the truth and knowing know we know?

Courteous of manners, in the liberal field,
    like Hughes' burnt fox, and bleeding, we have come
Fighting our corners, until the truth's revealed.
    It is the pain to which we did not succumb.
O all along the sea no other grace will do,
    I am your chance companion and our meeting true.

On The Labours Of A Literary Friend

Heavenly Father, full of grace,
    donor of marriage, calculus, and loss of face,
Reach down, as you tread
    the terracotta floors of heaven,
To cushion this philosophic man
    and the giant forms of his mind,
As he ponders the air
    in the pipe smoke of his study.
Balance him, as he beats
    a path around
The blue bay of Brixham,
    the parabolic gulls

The lines of verse
    in the lyrical tabernacle
Of his eyes. Ease him
    into the kitchen of his wife,
The noble Patricia,
    the singing screen of her word processor
Upstairs in her study,
    the breakfast toast
Nothing unusual, as they hear,
    Heavenly Father, your auditory
Footsteps on the stair
    of your open palace.

Wave them in, as they age.
    Do not stint
On the red wine and the sandwiches
    I know you have in abundance
In the rocking beulah of your treasury.
    See, there, the tamarisk,
The riverside rowboat, and the myrtle
    joyous with praise
In the doxology of the air,
    because they understand William
And all his works
    are coming home today.

Be there, champions
    of the mind, philosophers,
Poets with an ounce
    of civet up the snout.
Praise him, Loreleis
    of the arabesque, sexual equations
Of the dragonfly,
    dumb oxen of the golden plough.
For into the cognizance of certainty
    a lover of life
Inherits the aquamarine living room
    of a poet's paradise.

For Eddie Linden On His 70th Birthday

The sprawl of language is the less
For what you are and I address,
Dear editor, my Eddie, who,
Shacked up in Sutherland Avenue,
Published four decades of verse
Uniquely in *Aquarius*.
No one knows how you became
The man behind the Christian name.
Or do we know? For what you are,
Like the formation of a star,
Comes into being like the sun
Closer now your work is done,
And we see what you always were,
An incandescent Irish seer
Toppling the icons of an age
On a microscopic wage,
Drunk as the sea where Skellig sails
All night the black Atlantic gales.
Seventy years, and now the face
Of granite obstacles in place,
Like love and death and bowel cancer
Erasing any easy answer.
So face the truth and face it well
My perfect friend in asphodel.

For Glyn Hughes On His 70th Birthday

A little love within the eye
Becomes the one I see you by.
Dear Glyn, let me entice you round
To drink, where ruby wine is found
A droplet in a piece of glass
As lucid as a loving face.
And if we wonder by what rite
This wine is sacred, take tonight.
It is the rite to be alive
And, being man or woman, give
The perfect honour of our praise,
To crush the pain and wasted days
Recovered from the common lot,
The form and content of your art.

A little love within the eye
Becomes the one I see you by.
So close your eyes and, honoured, dream,
Sweet Mary is my hidden theme.
She visits you in such a vision
You meet her in a rich collision,
For, like a woman fleshed with God,
She glorifies your dreaming head,
And in her arms (in night so dark
She generates our saviour's spark)
You feel her touch your forehead, where
Hope encapsulates despair,
And, like a man the Yorkshire Moors
Know inside out, this woman's yours.

The Bower Of Bliss
for Xanthi

A bower of bliss
    on a summer day,
Your school report
    and your sunny way,
You sure have taken
    my breath away.

Sparrows hop
    in the lacy shade,
The look on your face
    no man has made,
A joke or two
    the more it stayed.

Dream in the green
    and yellow light,
The silver leaves
    in the bright moonlight
Lasting through
    the summer night.

The unheard music
    in the street
Gave our hearts
    a single beat.
We heard it and
    we felt complete.

I made this song
    for you, for you
Made my summer
    dream come true,
Down to earth
    and on it too.

Jubilee 2002

Majesty threw at Buckingham Palace
    the mother of all garden parties.
On the roof hear Brian May
    on guitar plunder irony,
The national anthem played to sound
    the depths of royal common ground.

Do you see anyone in tears,
    in tax assault, or rent arrears?
Two hundred million watch, agape,
    as laws of sober bliss take shape.
I see it with my eyes and tell
    the story that I love so well.

The Queen of England sits up straight
    through songs of ecstasy of state,
None so vocal as the one
    the living Paul McCartney sang,
All you need is love, to burn
    inside the thorax of the dawn.

No liquid daylight rich as that
    in which this love is where it's at.
Give me a draught of Aussie wine,
    I'll tell you why the soul's divine.
In every face I meet, who knows
    the love of reverence, she goes.

The gypsies dance, the bikers groove.
    No judgment is so fair as love.
In treaty with the cynics, I
    write this contract on the sky.
Release my praise, and let it be
    old England young in jubilee.

Larkin

Larkin plays the knowing man,
    the one who knows it all.
He's like a clever can
    superior to a football.
He saw his whole vocation
    derived from deprivation,
More money in the bank
    than a global-trotting yank,
Not begging for a penny
    like a man who hasn't any.
The clever bit, however, is
    he plays the poet too,
The knowing man who nonetheless
    knows poetry is true.

Well, not quite true, not quite a lie,
    a shy sophistication
I take upon myself and why
    risk an explanation?
The knowing man, who knows it all,
    would, of course, I realise,
Avoid the rather complex hassle,

    nor mess with truth nor mess with lies.
Like a bull in a china shop,
    I didn't know when to stop.
I knew it all, the sick deceit,
    the cabbage patch where Milton fell,
The difference (it's an old conceit)
    between true heaven and lying hell.

O the knowledge of the poet,
    who knew enough to duck it,
Who knew enough to blow it,
    but not enough to fuck it.

Dickhead

Dickhead pissing on the truth,
    give yourself a break.
Many a cowboy wears a suit,
    but none so false unique.

There is more classic rodeo
    in horses on the screen
Ridden by honest men who know
    your politics obscene.

The Burial Of The Christian Hypocrites

Daily the news is the same for me,
    murder of Jews in the first degree.
Hear my poem, O generous friend,
    not for the squeamish, nor meant to offend.

Two millennia of Christian lore
    sowed the seeds of the Hitler war.
Bishops went crazy, but Hitler said,
    'The Christian religion wishes them dead.

I'll tell you what, I'll kill them all,
    and the Christian hypocrites as well.'
Nobody noticed the last little phrase
    as Christians forked the Jews to the blaze.

Nobody noticed as mountains of ash
    buried the Christians under the cross.

A Song For Saint Peter

Put me to bed and let me sleep.
    Dig me a grave and dig it deep.
I'm sick to my teeth of the daily chores.
    I'm sick to my death of the daily wars.

Build me a birdman, let me fly
    far far away with a wink in my eye.
Show me the throne on chromium wheels
    and just how the entertainment feels.

Prostrate me before the fiery shrine.
    Fix me up with a glass of wine.
Guide me around the good and the wise.
    Tender me gently the rich supplies.

Put me to bed with my wife and I
    like a man of sense will soundly die.

What The Statues Saw

Lost in a dream in a foreign land,
    I came to a town where a river flows
Under a bridge, where the statues stand,
    sculpted from granite, God only knows.

The sky was a wall of water, the air
    its sluice to the river, the river the roar,
The race to the place, where the statues stare,
    grounded in granite, petrified awe.

The land was a forest lost in the sea,
    the sea was an ocean nobody sails.
A star in the heavens seemed happy to be
    witness when civilisation fails.

I woke in a whirlwind, sweating in bed,
    senseless in safety, rubbing my eyes.
The future's a rainbow over the dead
    clothing the statues posthumously wise.

Drops On A Thread

Early morning curls the blue
    transcendental sky
to the weightless word.

I drink the lucubrations
    of devoutly fragrant
exegesis.

The joy of art
    is the play of truth
on the red river of reason.

God gives us wisdom,
    like sand on the seashore,
on which we sunbathe, sleep.

On the immense altitude
    of my towering ignorance,
I pray.

Poisoned by envy for the world's esteem,
    I was a lamp of God
snuffed.

The Basque beggar saint advised,
    'Laugh and grow strong,
Humility is truth.'

Terrible as truth, I am
    a house of prayer
in radiant rain.

On the tip of modernity
    I hear
the anamnesis of is.

Don't weep for me when I am gone.
    I lie here dead
flying in the bone.

When Do You Sleep?

When a blackbird sings in a leafless tree,
And the sun shines wild on the earthly city;

When a crocus opens in the ground of night,
And a squirrel leaps through his own delight

Tumbling under *The Alchemist* rose;
When my silent office seeks to appraise

The glory of God in the mind of man;
When the files are closed and the long day's done,

And the sun takes leave through its misty chill;
When darkness descends on Stamford Hill,

And the tired return by the light of the stars,
And the hearth of home and the heart are theirs;

When my wife sleeps sweet in her bower of bliss,
And the black night's rich with her goodnight kiss;

When the true Christ walks on the sea of blood,
That's when I sleep, O my Lord and my God.

Untitled

There is no place in which I have not been.
Deep in the doom of death I die alone.
I am the place in which all places meet.

I am the ghost in the living dead machine.
I am the clear white light in the dying bone.
I've sat and chatted with the rich élite.

Before the rocks were molten I was there.
I am the summer in a woman's eye.
Vast as the sea I am the unwept tear.

There is no forest, there is no desert air,
There is no bed, in which I do not die.
I am the cloisters in which the monks appear.

There is no place in which I have not been.
I've sat and chatted with the rich élite.
I am the ghost in the living dead machine.
I am the place in which all places meet.

Spirit Of The River

Goodbye, my friends,
    the sunset on the leaf,
The stars at night,
    are time, the suttle theef.

The gorgeous trees
    inspire the painters blood,
Visionary intellectuals
    rooted in the mud.

The wind within the abbey
    five hundred years decay
Sounds with running water
    where the flautists play.

The solemn river
    swollen with the rain
Transports the tidy ducks
    to northern Spain.

Goodbye, my friends,
    I'm learning how to go
Where time runs down to silence
    the full fantastic show.

Notes to 'Spirit Of The River'

54. 'Springtime In The Greek Mountains'. The poem is set in a house I built in the mountain village of Sitochorion in Messinias in the south west Peloponnese. *Hughes' burnt fox* refers to 'The Burnt Fox' in *Winter Pollen* by Ted Hughes (Faber 1994). The fox came to him in a dream, humanoid and charred, as though burnt in a fire. It put its burnt, bleeding paw on an essay he was writing. 'Stop this, you are destroying us,' it said, leaving a bloody print on the paper. The fox may be thought of as a harbinger of the grace of poetry.

56. 'On The Labours Of A Literary Friend'. William Oxley. With his wife Patricia Oxley, editor of the literary magazine *Acumen*.

58. 'For Eddie Linden On His 70th Birthday'. *Sutherland Avenue* in Maida Vale in London. *Skellig*, Skellig Michael, a pyramid of rock 200 metres high 12 kilometres west of County Kerry in Ireland, the westernmost point of Britain. Following the established monastic tradition in Christendom, a monastery was founded on the rock, *c.* 6th century, and was active for over 600 years. The beehive cells of stone remain intact. Living through the Atlantic gales was one of the survival skills of the monks. *Skellig* is here a symbol of Eddie Linden's survival skill as a literary editor. *bowel cancer*, he survived it.

71. 'Drops On A Thread'. *The Basque beggar saint*, Ignatius Loyola (*c.* 1491-1556), founder of the Jesuits. *The anamnesis of is* refers to the not-forgetting or the re-remembering of being, as this was understood by the Greeks and the Israelites.

73. 'Spirit Of The River'. *suttle theef*, John Milton (1608-1674) in his sonnet, 'How soon hath Time the suttle theef of youth, / Stoln on his wing my three and twentith yeer!'